Love Grams

60 HILARIOUS DO-IT YOURSELF LOVE LETTERS TO FILL IN AND SEND OUT

HARVEY RACHLIN

A Perigee Book

*Dedicated with all my love
and affection to Alice ("Smooch"),
who is elegantly beautiful,
outrageously sexy,
and divinely romantic.*

Perigee Books
are published by
The Putnam Publishing Group
200 Madison Avenue
New York, New York 10016

Copyright © 1983 by Harvey Rachlin
All rights reserved. This book, or parts thereof,
may not be reproduced in any form without permission.
Published simultaneously in Canada by
General Publishing
Co. Limited, Toronto.

Library of Congress Cataloging in Publication Data

Rachlin, Harvey.
   Love grams.

   1. Letter-writing—Anecdotes, facetiae, satire,
etc. 2. Love-letters. I. Title.
PN6231.L44R3   1983   816'.54   82-19054
ISBN 0-399-50719-1

BOOK DESIGN BY BERNARD SCHLEIFER

First Perigee Printing, 1983

Printed in the United States of America

1 2 3 4 5 6 7 8 9

Contents

	Introduction	5
LETTER	TITLE	
1	The Highbrow's Billet-Doux	7
2	The "Morning After" Love Letter	9
3	College Girl's Letter to Her Mother	11
4	The Lawyer's Love Letter	13
5	The Enthusiastic Love Letter	15
6	The "Moral" Girl's Love Letter	17
7	The Rating Love Letter	19
8	The Lazy Person's Love Letter	21
9	Soap Opera Fan's Love Letter	23
10	Letter to Leave on the Kitchen Table in the Morning Before Your Mate Awakes	25
11	Letter to Your Boyfriend or Girlfriend	27
12	Missing Person's Report	29
13	The Tease Love Letter	31
14	Letter to Improve Communication Between Lovers	33
15	The Aggressive Person's Love Letter	35
16	The Poet's Love Letter	37
17	Valentine's Day Letter	39
18	The Song Lover's Love Letter	41
19	Love Letter from a Schizophrenic	43
20	The Search Warrant Love Letter	45
21	Letter That Will Help a New Relationship Blossom	47
22	My First Time	49
23	The Puzzle Love Letter	51
24	The Doctor's Love Letter	53
25	The Moron's Love Letter	55
26	The "What My Parents Think of You" Letter	57
27	The "I Appreciate You" Love Letter	59
28	The Horny Person's Love Letter	61

29	Lover's License	63
30	The Seductive Love Letter	65
31	Let's Mate on Our Date	67
32	The Die-Hard's Love Letter	69
33	Letter to Give to Your Mate on Your Wedding Day	71
34	The Gay Love Letter	73
35	The "Say 'I Love You'" Love Letter	75
36	Lover's Ticket	77
37	The Fairy Tale Love Letter	79
38	Love Letter to a Celebrity	81
39	The Marriage Proposal Love Letter	83
40	Woman's Response to a Marriage Proposal	85
41	The Questionnaire Love Letter	87
42	The Nighttime Love Letter	91
43	The Romantic Love Letter	93
44	Love Letter to a Guy Who Becomes Cheap	95
45	A Single Person's Love Letter to a Non-Expressive Partner	97
46	The "Fruity" Person's Love Letter After the First Sexual Experience	99
47	Letter to Your Secret Lover	101
48	Love Letter to Use After an Argument	103
49	The Lusty Guy's Love Letter	105
50	The Ego-Booster Love Letter	107
51	The Suggestive Love Letter	109
52	The Smitten Person's Letter	111
53	Love Letter to Give to Someone on the Street Whom You Are Attracted To	113
54	The Mae West Love Letter	115
55	Letter to a Jewish Mother	117
56	The Stop-Playing-Games Love Letter	119
57	Getting Your Lover to Change	121
58	The Real Man's Letter	123
59	The "Love at First Sight" Letter	125
60	Woman's Letter to a Lecher	127

INTRODUCTION

DID YOU EVER want to mesmerize that perfect "10" with passionate prose? Did you ever consider altering your pickup technique from lines that invariably come out sounding like macho clichés? Are you so enraptured that saying "I love you" seems an infinitesimal description of your emotions?

For the hopelessly smitten, the desperately enamored, and the furiously infatuated, intimate relief can be found in the words of the love letter. The prescriptions to satisfy your romantic needs are offered in this book.

It is hoped that *Love Grams* may serve you in a couple of ways. First, that it will provide entertainment for you and dish up some chuckles. And, second, that it will be an incentive for you enamored souls to sit down and write romantic prose to someone (hopefully, this will result in your receiving some back). Exchanging romantic correspondence is fun and can even make a relationship—new or old—more interesting.

Love Grams is a "do-it-yourself" love letter book. The letters have been designed for you to use by filling someone's name in the salutation, and, in many instances, by filling in blank spaces to personalize them. Then you can simply cut them out along the black line and send them to your loved one(s). You are encouraged to use these letters or variations of them (you can make changes to adapt them). Perhaps you will be inspired to write your own funny letters. Be creative. There is no end to the originality that can go into writing love letters. Do not just pour your heart out. Show that underneath that romantic soul lies a fine sense of humor. Sprinkle your letters with "cute" things that only you and your amour would understand—pet names, expressions, places you've been to, experiences you've shared, anecdotes. The use of these elements in funny settings will surely melt any heart.

You can also have some extra belly laughs with "Love Letter to a Celebrity," "The Nighttime Love Letter" and "The Romantic Love Letter." Ask your lover for nouns, verbs and adjectives to go in the blank spaces. Then write them in and read the letters aloud.

There can be unlimited fun and gratification in writing and exchanging billets-doux. Love letters are to keep, and in good form they can do no worse than bring a smile, excise a laugh, or warm the heart of the recipient. At best, they can . . . well . . . try it and find out for yourself!

ACKNOWLEDGMENTS

IN COMPLETING THIS BOOK I am grateful to the following:

My editor, Judy Linden, who had the foresight, intuition, savvy, or whatever it is that makes an editor great, to take a basic idea and shape it into the final product it now is. Judy is not only brilliant at what she does, but is the cutest editor I have ever met;

My agent, Lynn Seligman, who believed in this project from the very beginning and saw it through. Lynn is terrifically inspiring and is truly an "agent's agent";

My brother, Steven Rachlin, who helped nurture this book from conception and who provided many creative ideas;

My brother, Craig Rachlin, a young man with a flair for romance and comedy who also provided many inventive ideas;

My typist, Margaret Dyke, whose role goes well beyond that of typist. Ideas were bounced off her and she made numerous invaluable suggestions;

My friend Lou Stevens, for his suggestions;

My parents, Philip and Mazie Rachlin, and brother Gary, sisters-in-law Sharon and Jeanne, my future mother-in-law Naomi and sisters-in-law, Sara French and Susan Westfried, and Diane Cozzi, Stanley Barkan, Agnes Dubin, Sally Shiller, Pearl Bernstein, Elliott Miller, Bonnie Schachter, Teresa Jucha, Amy J. Browne, and Lois Pike, who all have a wonderful sense of humor and enduring patience.

The Highbrow's Billet-Doux

Saalam _____,

I am solicitous regarding my cerebral welfare. It appears that I am unable to ruminate about anything except you. It is conventional for a person who is smitten to fixate upon his or her consort, but not to the great measure I do of you. Invariably when I gaze the apparition of your visage is upon me, all scents that my proboscis respires are reminiscent of your essence, all with whom I have interlocution, I address by your appellation. I savor you in my comestibles, osculate torridly with you in my subconscious nocturnal visions, construe in perusing my literary oeuvres that you are the subject of the motifs. Comparatively, a typical forlorn individual seems salubrious.

Cognizant that I am possessed of these indisposed musings, it is incumbent upon me to seek succor. The expedient accomodation would be an institution where they minister to the non compos mentis. I shall matriculate, and should they petition for a diagnosis, I shall simply enunciate that I am a veritable philo_____iac!
NAME OF LOVED ONE*

*If name is more than one syllable, use first syllable only, except where first syllable is only one letter, in which case you end with the first following consonant (e.g. Amy, philoamiac). Always try to end with a consonant; if last letter is a vowel, drop it (Examples: philophiliac (Philip), philojudiac (Judy), philojohniac (John)).

Translation: The Intellectual's Love Letter

Dear _____,

    I am deeply concerned about my mental health. I seem not to be able to concentrate on anything but you. It is natural for someone in love to be preoccupied with his or her mate, but not to the extent I am of you. Everywhere I look I see your face, everything I breathe smells like you, everyone I talk to I call by your name. I taste you in my food, make-out with you in my dreams, read about you in my books. I make a regular lovesick person seem healthy.

    Aware that I have these sick thoughts, I feel it is necessary for me to seek attention. The proper facility would be an institution where they treat the insane. I shall check in, and should they ask the reason for my being there, I shall simply say that I am literally crazy about you!

The "Morning After" Love Letter

TIME MAGAZINE   PLAYBOY   COSMOPOLITAN
THE NEW YORK TIMES   NEWSWEEK

_____ PUTS ON COMMAND PERFORMANCE
_{MATE'S NAME}

PROMISING CAREER FOR RISING NEW STAR

Last night this critic was treated to an exhilarating, dazzling and titillating performance that will indubitably rank high in the annals and glories of "evening pastimes." This unique three-act-play, authored, directed, produced, and performed by _____,
_{NAME OF PARTNER}
marks the emergence on the scene of a skillful and lusty trouper.

The drive and energy of _____
_{MISS/MRS.}
_____ is demonstrated immediately
_{LAST NAME}
after the male star rises. Within minutes _____
_{HE/SHE}
conveys that rare blend of ineffable magic that few performers can conjure up. The show's most delicious moment occurs when _____ _____
_{MR./MISS/MRS.}   _{LAST NAME}
does the ramming routine, which might be said to be . . . tongue in chic.

The score was at once buoyant and brash. This was probably the high point of the show. For each lifting number there would follow a period of tranquility and comic relief.

To say that _____ _____ moved with passionate frenzy is as much an understatement as to say that a dog in heat is lethargic. The only criticism that might be given here is that the stage floor squeaked, but somehow one cannot help but get the feeling that this just goes with the ambience of such a play.
_{MR./MISS/MRS.}   _{LAST NAME}

While it is true that this was not _____ _____'s first outing in this part, _____ played it with such panache that it is less a revival than more a classic comeback.
_{MR./MISS/MRS.} _{LAST NAME} _{HE/SHE}

The show may not be perfect family entertainment, but any mature adult could appreciate its vitality. Tickets are going to be hard to get as the theater is intimate and holds only a limited audience.

This "show" differed from conventional plays in various respects. Unlike traditional plays, the second and third acts didn't begin at specified intervals. Half the excitement was just wondering if there were going to be subsequent acts. Both were certainly well worth the wait though (the performance improved and the acts became longer as the evening progressed). There was almost a fourth act to this play but the star fell asleep.

It was truly an exhausting performance, but now that the leading _____ has had time to rest and recoup strength through the night, it is this critic's craving that _____ _____ would give an encore.
_{MAN/LADY}   _{MR./MISS/MRS.} _{LAST NAME}

Right now!

P.S. Stop smiling and get over here!

College Girl's Letter to Her Mother

Dear Mom,

You wouldn't believe how wild the kids are at this school. Everybody's really into partying and having good times. I'm having lots of fun too—_____ has opened up a whole
NAME OF COLLEGE
new world of pleasurable experiences for me.

Remember those long talks that you, me, and Daddy had before I left? How I'm still a young girl and should put my studies first and not get involved at my young age. Well, Mom, there comes a time in every girl's life that she must become a woman, if you know what I mean. I don't know how to say this without exciting you. I've thought it over and over and have come to the conclusion that I just have to be blunt and tell the truth.

Yes . . . I did it. At first I didn't want to, but then everyone in my dorm practically had done it, and I was maybe the only one left. The pressure was unbearable. It's not that I had to go along with the group—you know, be a follower. It was just something I wanted to do. I was curious. I heard so much about it that I just had to try it.

And you know what? I love it. I really love it. Please don't be upset, but it's been the most satisfying experience of my life, and I plan to actively participate for the remainder of my college years.

I'm no longer your little girl, Mom. I'm a woman now.

I joined a sorority.

The Lawyer's Love Letter

DISTRICT COURT OF THE
COUNTY OF _____

           COUNTY

SUBPOENA FOR A DATE

_____, Esq.
YOUR NAME
   Plaintiff   Index No. _____
                       NUMBER
    v.

_____
DATE'S NAME
   Defendant

YOU ARE HEREBY SUMMONED to appear at _____, _____, at _____, on _____ _____ _____ for a very special and romantic evening—great food, fine conversation and humor, and the best in company. Reasons for this subpoena appear below. You must answer this request within one week of receipt of this letter; upon your failure to answer, judgment will be taken against you for the "relief" demanded in a subsequent complaint.

 NOTE: The law provides that:
 (a) any unreasonable excuse given with respect to the above action will result in the severest penalties allowed;
 (b) any excuse is unreasonable.

CHARGES

Plaintiff alleges as follows:

FIRST CAUSE OF ACTION:
1. Plaintiff is attractive and huggable
2. Plaintiff is sexy and mysterious
3. Plaintiff is generous and funny
4. Plaintiff is romantic and has good taste

SECOND CAUSE OF ACTION:
1. Defendant is adorable and lovable
2. Defendant is sensual and intriguing
3. Defendant is kind and witty
4. Defendant is charming and delicious

THIRD CAUSE OF ACTION:

It's a perfect match!

WHEREFORE, Plaintiff demands judgment against Defendant for one date to see if they are as compatible as his instincts tell him.

Date: _____, _____.   Signed,
      DATE OF THIS LETTER   YEAR

                                                      _____
                                                      YOUR NAME, PLAINTIFF

The Enthusiastic Love Letter

Dear _____,

I've flipped over you! So don't expect me to be upright all the time. I'm topsy-turvy, head over heels over the greatest _____ in the world!
GUY/GAL

The "Moral" Girl's Love Letter

Dear _____,

Hear ye, hear ye, hear ye. Let it be known that I, _____, being of sound mind and pristine values, hereby declare that I socialize under a "moral code" that must be strictly abided by and adhered to at all times. Violation of any of these orders will result in the "death sentence."
_{YOUR NAME}

_____'s Ten Commandments of Propriety:
_{YOUR NAME}

1. Thou shalt first requesteth a goodnight kiss before making any such attempt. Furthermore, no tongues!
2. Thou shalt not touch my private parts with thy Russian hands and Roman fingers (at least not without my express prior consent).
3. Thou shalt pervade thy speech with wholesome language (I am also impressed with erudite wisdom); gutter language of any kind is taboo.
4. Be chivalrous in your manners: say "please," "may I," "excuse me," and "thank you"; open and close the car door for me; and don't ever lose your temper. Treat me with courtesy, honor, and respect, for to be in my company is a privilege which must constantly be earned.
5. Thy breath and armpits shall always be fresh-smelling. Thou shalt always shower before seeing me and regularly wash out thy mouth.
6. Thou shalt never fabricate any untruths about me or our relationship to any third party, particularly about my honor.

7. Thou shalt not covet other beautiful women in my presence (I shouldest be enough!).
8. Thou shalt enter my home after a date by my express invitation only. Thou shalt not try to coerce or smooth-talk me into such invitation and under no circumstances will thou ever be invited when in an intoxicated state.
9. Thou shalt always requesteth the presence of my company no less than _____NUMBER_____ days in advance of the requested engagement. Occasional exceptions allowed.
10. Thou shalt go alongeth with all my requests and decisions. Thou shalt not question my behavior or attempt to understandeth anything seemingly irrational.

P.S. If thou abideth by this crock of shit, then thou shouldest have thy head examined!

The Rating Love Letter

Dear _____,

    Hollywood gave Bo Derek a "10," but on my scale she would have received a "_____." You see, I have impeccable standards. Now, my dear, I give you the honor of being rated by me. Keep in mind that what's generally perfect for anybody else is only average to me!
_{NUMBER}

    The Rating of _____
_{NAME}
(Ratings are based on the usual scale of 1 to 10, 1 being the lowest and 10 being the highest possible score.)

(Please turn letter)

Face Rating:	Preciousness Rating:	Vivaciousness Rating:
Body Rating:	Tenderness Rating:	Ambition Rating:
Brains Rating:	Affectionateness Rating:	Loyalty Rating:
Personality Rating:	Intuitiveness Rating:	Passion Rating:
Sensitivity Rating:	Magnetism Rating:	Kisses Rating:
Nature Rating:	Creativity Rating:	Cuddles Rating:
Humbleness Rating:	Sense of humor Rating:	Sexiness Rating:
Charm Rating:	Wittiness Rating:	Horniness Rating:
Consideration Rating:	Earthiness Rating:	Lovemaking Rating:
Generosity Rating:	Mysteriousness Rating:	Kinkiness Rating:
		OVERALL RATING:

SCORING:

250–300 Too perfect to be believed
200–249 Hot stuff
150–199 Member in good standing
100–149 Three months' probation
50–99   Don't call me, I'll call you
0–49   My condolences

The Lazy Person's Love Letter

Dear _____,

    Ah-h-h-h-h-h (yawn) love you. Z — Z — Z — Z — Z — Z — Z — Z — Z — Z — Z — Z — Z — Z — Z — Z — Z

Soap Opera Fan's Love Letter

Dear _____,

Years ago, when I was YOUNG AND RESTLESS, I always knew as sure AS THE WORLD TURNS that one day I would find someone like you—someone who would be my GUIDING LIGHT and _____ ALL MY CHILDREN. I
_{HAVE/FATHER}
always felt that tomorrow would be the day I would find you. Well, my SEARCH FOR TOMORROW ended the day I met you.

The first time I saw you, I thought I had entered ANOTHER WORLD. It was wonderful the way we spent the DAYS OF OUR LIVES together, and I especially enjoyed the quiet evenings as we walked until the EDGE OF NIGHT.

But yesterday I felt as if my world had ended when I heard that you had left for TEXAS. I went straight to THE DOCTORS to see if anything could be done for me. They rushed me to _____ GENERAL HOSPITAL and
_{NAME OF COUNTY}
placed me in the care of a top specialist. Dr. RYAN'S HOPE for me was that if you returned immediately, I might still have ONE LIFE TO LIVE.

Letter to Leave on the Kitchen Table in the Morning Before Your Mate Awakes

Dear _____,

You looked so cute this morning when you were sleeping that as I got out of bed and watched you, I was smiling brightly. I can just imagine how adorable you were as a little tot. Did you know how adorable you would be one day as a big tot?

Life goes by really fast. It seems like one day you're a kid and the next day you're a grownup. We work so hard all the time to better our lives that sometimes we don't take time out to appreciate what we have. I'm sure glad I have you to go through adult life with.

We have been through so much together. And there's a lot more to go. I look forward to this and will cherish each day as it comes. You know, we really have come to know each other in a special way. I think that's because you're such a special person. If I haven't told you lately how much I love you and adore you and cherish you, then I'm saying it now.

I hope your day is as bright as you have made mine!

Letter to Your Boyfriend or Girlfriend

Dear _____,

It is with great humbleness that I have the honor of addressing the eminent, exalted, fabulous, venerable, and impeccable _____. Allow my in-
FULL NAME
dulgence in extolling someone I so very much admire, and who is not only the most wonderful _____
BOY/GIRLFRIEND
in this town, but also this state, this country, and this world (including any extraterrestrials!).

Your virtues are as diverse as your greatness excels over the human race. In the highest sense of these words, you are kind, intelligent, warm, understanding and, yes, ever so _____. Oh, I am just
HANDSOME/BEAUTIFUL
green with jealousy when we are together in public for I know that all _____ eyes are upon you, craving
MALE/FEMALE
for the taste of your lips, the touch of your body. You are the greatest _____ of all time, the
STUD/"MAN-IPULATOR"
_____ of eternity, the sex idol of
DON JUAN/CLEOPATRA
_____. Yet you be a mortal, you possess sen-
MEN/WOMEN
sitivity and angelic goodness unprecedented in mankind. You contain a passion for living, real genius, and esoteric tastes that we common people cannot fully comprehend, no less appreciate in its entirety. Forgive us for our human failings, almighty Allah, and accept our gratitude for enlightening mankind with your supreme presence.

Okay, you can come down from your cloud now. Actually, this letter is just to say hello, bring a smile to your face, and make you feel good. I also would like you to know that I think you're a wild and craaaaaaazy _____. And I love you.
      GUY/GAL

Missing Person's Report

All Points Bulletin!!!

Attention all cars! _____ has re-
                          YOUR NAME
ported that a very special person has been missing for
_____ _____. The missing person is iden-
  NUMBER   HOURS/DAYS/MONTHS
tified as _____ of _____,
              FULL NAME   ADDRESS
_____. _____ was last seen in the
  CITY OR TOWN   HE/SHE
vicinity of _____. Please give this case
                    PLACE
your maximum priority. It is imperative that _____
                                              LOVER'S FIRST NAME
and _____ be reunited at once.
     YOUR FIRST NAME

Information to Help Find the Missing Person

Height:_____ Personality description:_____
Weight:_____ Most outstanding features:_____
Eye color:_____ Favorite places:_____
Hair color:_____ Closest relative or friend:_____
                         Profession:_____
                         Employer:_____
                         Address:_____
                         Favorite card game:_____
                         Favorite magazines:_____
                         Favorite recording artists:_____

                         Favorite foods:_____
                         Description of person's kisses:_____
                         _____

                         Horniest moments:_____
                         Visible body marks:_____
                         Education (last school
                             attended):_____

Sketch of_____   Person(s) who might want to
           NAME   kidnap victim:_____

The Tease Love Letter

My Dearest _____,

Last night was so exciting I just had to thank you with this letter. Never in my whole life have I been with a man as equal in physical prowess as you.

You were the conqueror in what people commonly regard as only a recreation. Having expected only an average encounter, I never dreamed it would be so much fun. That's because of what you put into it—you have that rare but natural gift. Your upstrokes were long and hard, your downstrokes smooth but gentle.

You never tired. You were relentless in your desire to enjoy the evening as much as possible. I was overwhelmed by your erect posture and strength, calculating each move as only a man with years of experience could do. And what style! You gripped your club so carefully each time before making your thrustful "swing." I must admit that after the first twenty minutes I could hardly catch my breath—but how could I disappoint your unquenchable appetite for more?

My only complaint was that you insisted on keeping score. Who cares what's par for the course anyway? Wasn't it enough just to enjoy yourself for the sport? Anyway, no big thing. I never saw anyone go at it with such vigor and passion. Besides, you were most kind in letting me wash your balls afterward. You're just the partner I've always been looking for.

Whenever you want to play miniature golf again, don't hesitate to call me.

Letter to Improve Communication Between Lovers

Dear _____,

    Wehavebeenhavingalackofcommunicationlatelysoi thoughtiwouldwritealettertoyouthiswayyouseeithought ifyoucouldunderstandthisletterthenyoucouldcompre hendanythingiwantedtotellyouandwhatihavetosayis veryimportantsoreadcarefullyiloveyoubearinmindmy dearthatmerewordscannotexpresstheintensityofmylove northedepthofmyemotionsortheheightofmyjoynomatter whatpleasebelievethisithinkcommunicationisveryimpor tantandhopethatthistangledletterwillserveasastimulusin thefutureforbetterandmorefrequentintercourse.

The Aggressive Person's Love Letter

Dear _____,

    Beware! This is to inform you that I have officially declared "war" on you, and the next time we meet you should be prepared for some savage warfare. I have an arsenal of weapons at my disposal, including bun guns, cum-spears, muff muskets, dork daggers, dildo bilbos, cherrybombs, pecker wreckers, schwein popguns, milky way missles, and cooz bazookas. And these are just my backup weapons.

    I shall begin this "war" by dropping some 20-megaton kisses on you. These are powerful devices known to weaken the victim and in some cases render her helpless. This will be followed by my Nookie Hand Grenades. These are two five-fingered tentacles which probe the victim's vulnerable areas. They investigate strategic positions for a while and try to leave the victim paralyzed but still very much alive. (They seek out booby traps!) Next my Friction Fireball will be exploded. This is where tremendous heat from my palms is released so that you will be so hot that you will have to disrobe. Finally, my ultimate secret weapon, the Peter Torpedo will be engaged. This is a deadly weapon that expands in dark tunnels until it finally detonates. It is known to render its victims into wild ecstasy and is thus considered deadly.

I don't mind telling you my strategy, as any defense you implement will be rendered defenseless!

The Poet's Love Letter

When I was just a little __GIRL__
                                BOY/GIRL
I dreamed one day I'd find
A very special person who
Was __5'10"__ and kind
     HEIGHT
__Blonde__-colored hair __He'd__ have
 COLOR   HE'D/SHE'D
And be a(n) __Man__ by profession
            PROFESSION
Who'd look at me with eyes of __brown__
                                      COLOR
And whose __Buns__ would be my obsession
              BODY PART
You are __Romantic__ and __Handsome__
           QUALITY*   QUALITY
And you're __Sexy__ most of all
        QUALITY
That's why when we're together
__Sharon__ has a ball
FEMALE'S NAME

I could only love someone named __Greg__
                                              MATE'S FIRST NAME
Darling, yes it's true
That's why I give __Myself__ so freely
                        PHYSICAL ACT (PLURAL)
That someone I love is you!

*Grab bag of qualities: wonderful, passionate, delightful, adorable, affectionate, sensitive, charming, suave, refined, precious, huggable, tender, erotic, ambitious, funny, witty, understanding, sexy, amorous, romantic, bewitching, radiating, sensuous, elegant, beautiful, fantastic, magnetic, electrifying, intoxicating, devilish.

Valentine's Day Letter

Dear _____,

    Today is Valentine's Day, the celebration of love. Do you know the origin of this holiday? I think you should know because it relates to us in a special way. Let me tell you the story of this day of love.

    Valentine's Day originated over 1700 years ago in another part of the world. There was this Roman _____ who was in love with a local
_{YOUR PROFESSION}
_____. The _____,
_{RECIPIENT OF LETTER'S PROFESSION}   _{YOUR PROFESSION}
_____io was so cute
_{YOUR NAME (IF IT ENDS IN A VOWEL DROP LAST LETTER)}
that everyone called him "Cupid" as a nickname. But he was also very shy and lonely and wanted _____, the _____,
_{RECIPIENT OF LETTER}   _{RECIPIENT OF LETTER'S PROFESSION}
as his girlfriend. When Cupid found he wasn't getting anywhere with _____, he realized he
_{RECIPIENT OF LETTER}
needed to get her attention in a special way. So he devised a plan.

    On February 14th he would shoot an arrow through the air and into her buttocks, the tip endowed with an herbal serum believed to be a love potion. Greek legend had it that when a guy stuck his tip into a girl's rump she'd fall in love with him.

    The big day arrived and Cupid mounted his bow. As he drew back the arrow, his arm started quivering, sore from whacking his willy so much. He released the arrow prematurely, whereupon it flew through the air and missed the target, hitting her instead on the breast. All of a sudden water started trickling out, then oozing out, flooding the streets. All the men in town in beholding this sight ran over to her, vying for her attention (and perhaps a tasty lick). The fair maiden was obviously happy with her newfound popularity and didn't object to all the suckers.

Jealous, Cupid ran to _____ (RECIPIENT OF LETTER) and said that it was he who shot the arrow into her and that he should not have to share her with all the other men. She looked up at him and gently smiled. "But stupid Cupid," she said, "doesn't thou knowest? When tit rains, tit pours!"

The Song Lover's Love Letter

Dear _____,

"What's New Pussycat?" "I Couldn't Sleep a Wink Last Night." I just said "I'm Gonna Sit Right Down and Write Myself a Letter" to you. "You Were on My Mind." I was "Tossin' and Turnin'," "Thinking of You."

"Hey There," "Without You" "I Got Plenty O' Nuttin'." "I'm Lost Without Your Love" "You Sexy Thing," and when you're not "In the Mood" I think "You've Lost That Lovin' Feelin'." Ah, but "I Know" you have "Feelings" and "Love Will Keep Us Together."

"Baby Face," "I'd Really Love to See You Tonight." I "Got to Get You Into My Life" "More and More." "Tonight," "When the Moon Comes Over the Mountain," "Let's Get it On." "For Once in My Life," I'd like to "Rock Around the Clock," "Body and Soul" with a "Satin Doll." "Please Please Me." "Let the Good Times Roll" with "The Candy Man." It'll be real "Tutti Frutti." "After the Lovin'" we'll be "Happy Together."

"There's Something Nice About Everyone, But There's Everything Nice About You." "Great Balls of Fire," "You're the Cream in My Coffee." "You Are the Sunshine of My Life." "When You're Smiling" "Everything's Coming Up Roses." "Thank Heaven For Little Girls."

"P.S. I Love You."

Love Letter from a Schizophrenic

Dear _____,

    When I'm with you, it's like being in heaven. Your touch leaves me feeling high. When you run your hand through my hair, I get a tingling sensation. When you lay next to me, every part of me feels alive.

    It's great to have found someone wonderful like yourself. Having you really makes me feel as if I'm living. Just the thought of you leaves me elated. Whenever I picture you in my mind, I smile and think to myself, "I love you!"

Dear _____,

    When I'm with you, it's like being in hell. Your touch leaves me feeling low. When you run your hand through my hair, I get a headache. When you lay next to me, every part of me feels dead.

    It's disgusting to have found someone terrible like yourself. Having you really makes me feel as if I'm dying. Just the thought of you leaves me depressed. Whenever I picture you in my mind, I frown and think to myself, "I hate you!"

The Search Warrant Love Letter

Under the laws of the State of _____,
                                    YOUR STATE
_____, who is looking for _____,
  YOUR NAME   NOUN (LOVE, SEX, ETC.)
is duly authorized and commanded forthwith to diligently search _____, who is believed to possess
                        NAME
the desired "goods." _____ _____
                     MR./MISS/MRS.   YOUR LAST NAME
has just and reasonable cause to suspect and believe and does suspect and believe that said "goods" are concealed on this person.

On _____, _____ _____,
    NAME OF DAY   MONTH   DATE
_____ at _____, the two shall go to
   YEAR   TIME
_____ at _____, where
    PLACE   ADDRESS
_____ _____ will conduct an inquiry
MR./MISS/MRS. YOUR LAST NAME
relating to the physical and mental attributes of the suspect. At the end of the night, they will return to
_____'s home at _____ for the
  FIRST NAME   ADDRESS
"frisk." This will be a thorough search, so the suspect should be prepared to stay for a while and wear loose clothing to endure this long ordeal. The investigator will search any areas which might conceal the object of investigation: the belly button, armpits, ears, nostrils, and mouth.

45

If it has not been found at this point (you can be sure this part won't take too long), the search will get down to serious business, and the suspect will have to "assume the position." Any recalcitrance to this exploration may be immediately suppressed under law by the presentation of a copy of this search warrant. If said "goods" are found on the suspect, _____ will be dealt with ac-
                                HE/SHE
cording to law, _____'s law!
                    YOUR LAST NAME

Letter That Will Help a New Relationship Blossom

Dear _____,

We haven't been going together all that long, so before we get more involved, I thought there's something you ought to know about me. I've got this condition, you see. It's called "nice-_____-i-tis." It's a character disease whose victims have many symptoms. They are down-to-earth, warm, friendly, trusting, gentle, easygoing, good-natured, cheerful, and most of all, loving. I'm sure you can see that this affliction requires special handling.
_{GUY/GAL}

I am willing to entrust treatment of this illness to you. You seem to be the compassionate type, able to handle such a delicate situation. Besides, I have diagnosed you to have a case of "nice-_____-i-tis." Symptoms are exactly the same as described above.
_{GAL/GUY}

Nice-guy-i-tis and nice-gal-i-tis are actually complementary diseases whose only cure is that the victims be steady companions of one another. Not too many people contract these illnesses, so you should consider yourself lucky. Only special people get them. In the acute stage, they are long-term.

There are certain treatments prescribed for victims of our conditions. Rehabilitation includes going to movies, restaurants, parks, and beaches; moonlight walks and rides to the country have also been known to be therapeutic. Curiously, the better the treatment, the worse the symptoms grow. It is even rumored that couples who have had similar conditions developed a terminal condition: wedlock.

My First Time

Dear ~~Greg~~,

The first time I did it I was really just a babe in the woods. It happened rather fast—you know how these things are. But the first time for anybody is the one they remember the most, so let me tell you about it.

My partner in this experience was a person I loved very much and one with whom I spent all my time. This particular day we had been together for an hour or so; this other person had been touching and probing my private areas with much affection. It felt good. Real good. I remember finally getting this tingling sensation in my lower area. I knew I was ready to do it now, but funny as it seems, I wasn't sure how to do it. My partner, being more experienced, put me in the proper position. The urge became greater there, and after a few seconds I remember I "exploded." It shot out and I remember how good it felt. A few minutes later I cleaned up and got dressed.

That was how it happened the first time . . . my mother toilet trained me.

The Puzzle Love Letter

Dear _____,

There's something I'd like to tell you. It's difficult for me, being the way I am, to come right out and express myself, so I've made a cryptogram out of a quotation which sums up how I feel about you. A cryptogram is a group of words with new letters substituted for the real ones. You must decode the puzzle to determine the actual quote. It's not as hard as you think. So if you want to know how I feel about you, get to work on it right away!

Q JXZM IOMM—Q JXZM IOMM!
'IQP CJJ IOCI Q HCB PCF;
QI QP GF ZQPQXB QB IOM BQLOI,
GF RKMCGQBL QB IOM RCF.
—IOXGCP OXXR*

P.S. When we're together again, remind me to decode a personal message for you. It has plenty of XXXXX's in it!

*I love thee—I love thee!
'Tis all that I can say;
It is my vision in the night,
My dreaming in the day.
—Thomas Hood

The Doctor's Love Letter

Dear Ms._____,

Although I have been your personal physician for the past ten years, I have suppressed my true feelings toward you for professional reasons. Now, however, I find myself incapable of restraint and must divulge my deepest thoughts.

You are the most exciting patient I ever had the privilege of examining. Every time you stepped into my office, you sent chills up and down my spine—from my medulla oblongata to my conus medullaris. My heartbeat would accentuate until you could hear the residual systolic murmur I've had since birth. My temperature would soar to heights that normally would require immediate hospitalization and a spinal tap. Yes, my love, you did all these things to me and more.

Examining your chest always made me rise to the occasion. Remember the time I spent 3 hours looking for lumps in your breasts? Or how I so meticulously canvassed your buttocks with my hands looking for stretch marks? I have always believed in quality care. The pelvic exam was my favorite. Never did you twinge or clam up with excitement. You were always inviting like a true friend.

Somehow, I think you realized my delight in our doctor-patient relationship. Even though I never once violated my Hippocratic Oath and treated you as a sex object, you once pointed out that you never had a doctor before who seemed to obtain as much fulfillment from a physical examination as I. That's because you've made the art of practicing medicine truly a pleasure for this psychiatrist.

The Moron's Love Letter

Deer _____,

    Yoo no hoo ay am? Itz mee _____!

                                        YOUR NAME
Ay rite leters herdlee nevor, so dont hoap for this leter to sayound lik it wuz ritten bah a genyus.

    Ah juss wunted too seh thet ay lovs ya. I caint beegin to tel ya hal mooch. I caint bee thet stoopid if ay lovs ya, nal kud ay huhny?

    Yu shore am a swel peace of ass. Ay lov youre ass, boath haffs. Eaven wen yu face mee and ay caint c it. Ay luke forwood to sein it agen. Frum mah lipz too yawr behiny.

The "What My Parents Think of You" Letter

Dear _____,

    I'm glad you met my parents on _____. I know it was like going before the review board, but after all, they are my parents so their opinions are something I must live with. Following our date, both the CPO (chief petty officer, mother dear) and CFO (chief financial officer, daddy dearest) filed a report with me. I thought you would be interested in reading a candid analysis of their opinion of you. I have circled in the SRS (standard review sheet) that appears below, the response that most accurately reflects their opinion of you in each particular category.

        Review of _____
                                      DATE'S NAME

1. **First impression:**
   a. very, very nice
   b. let's set a wedding date
   c. subject to further examination
   d. "I don't trust this kid . . ."

2. **Personality:**
   a. bubbly
   b. very natural; must have been born with it
   c. like a barrel of monkeys
   d. needs a shot of cortisone

3. **Charm:**
   a. suave and debonair
   b. makes Cary Grant (Nancy Reagan) look like a nerd
   c. a real Don Juan (Lolita)
   d. couldn't charm a snake

4. **Manners:**
   a. must have graduated from West Point
   b. must have read "The Emily Post Book of Etiquette"
   c. could teach a course on it
   d. must have been drunk

5. **Sense of humor:**
   a. the next Johnny Carson (Joan Rivers)
   b. full of bons mots
   c. pleasantly subtle
   d. like white wine (dry but has the potential to ripen with age)

6. **Overall opinion:**
   a. can't stop talking about you
   b. my allowance has increased
   c. they love you
   d. they're taking me to a psychologist

The "I Appreciate You" Love Letter

Dear _____,

I just have to tell you how much I adore you. Ever since I met you it's been like Christmas every day. I never dreamed so many wonderful things could come in one package. I guess you can say I'm all wrapped up in you!

You're the greatest thing that ever happened to me. Now I know that's a very heavy remark but I wouldn't say it if it wasn't true. And if I wasn't as crazy about you as I am.

Yes my dear, I think you and I have a bright future together. The longer we know each other the better things seem to get. I want to always be there for you as I hope you'll always be there for me.

Keep up the Christmas spirit, and I'll show you the best Fourth of July fireworks display you ever saw!

The Horny Person's Love Letter

Dear _____,

Your beau, _____, has been under
YOUR NAME
scientific investigation for some time now and has been diagnosed to be suffering from an overabundance of lust for you. This is a potentially dangerous condition with a history of victims eventually succumbing to a state of wild and uncontrollable behavior if suitable remedies are not applied.

We have determined that the patient is entering phase two of this condition, and soon you will be observing various physical, behavioral and psychological symptoms: a dry mouth (from constant panting), wolf calls, constantly pursed lips, hands that can't keep to themselves, and the production of romantic designs on clothing (usually a heart-on). The medical profession implores you to render immediate and effective treatment for this sensitive patient. On the other side appears the prescriptions, which you can fill better than anyone else.

Rx for <u>SHARONS</u>'s condition:
YOUR NAME

One <u>KISS</u> twice each day.
　　　　NOUN

Two injections of <u>WANG</u> in the <u>TWAT</u>
　　　　　　　　　　NOUN　　　　　　　BODY PART
each morning.

Three bites on the <u>butt</u> each afternoon.
　　　　　　　　　　BODY PART

Five licks on the <u>CLIT</u> each night.
　　　　　　　　　BODY PART

In case of emergency, smother the patient with your
<u>Pelvis</u>.
BODY PART

　　　　　　　　　　　　　　　　　Respectfully,

　　　　　　　　　　　　　　　　　_____
　　　　　　　　　　　　　　　　　DR. I. FEELGOOD

Lover's License

Under the laws of the State of <u>Pennsylvania</u>, <u>Gregory</u> is hereby authorized
to be the devoted <u>Husband</u> of <u>Sharon</u>. The possession of this license is a privilege, and it must be utilized properly. Good behavior will result in rewards. The "point and reward system" appears below. Lover Identification No.: <u>1</u>

<u>6-21-66</u>   <u>Male</u>   <u>5'10"</u>   <u>Blue</u>   <u>Eternity</u>
DATE OF BIRTH   SEX   HEIGHT   EYES   DATE LICENSE EXPIRES

RESTRICTIONS (if any): <u>No S&M</u>

BEHAVIOR SYSTEM:
- ✓ considerateness (3)
- ✓ good-natured (5)
- ___ understanding (4)
- ✓ tender (2)
- ✓ charming (2)
- ✓ witty (3)
- ✓ huggable (1)
- ___ romantic (2)
- ___ loyal (5)
- ✓ affectionate (2)
- ✓ sensitive (1)
- ___ sexy (4)

REWARDS:
1-5 points—a movie (your choice)
6-15 points—a great big tongue kiss
16-28 points—dinner at your favorite restaurant
29 or more points—dessert

<u>Gregory W Chamberlain</u>
LOVER'S NAME

<u>RD1 Box 16</u>
ADDRESS

<u>Everett PA 15537</u>
CITY, STATE, ZIP CODE

<u>Sharon Chamberlain</u>
COMMISSIONER

(Sign your name)

The Seductive Love Letter

Dear _____,

I want _____ night to finally be the night
            DAY
that we let ourselves go and do everything we've always wanted (but chickened out to do in the past). I think it's ridiculous for us, two consenting adults, not to satisfy our desires. We do love each other, don't we? So if it's embarrassing, what should that matter.

I mean it when I say I want to do everything. Even if some strait-laced people would think what we'd be doing is "kinky," I don't care. It's the pleasure of the thing that counts, right? I know deep down that we both are burning with eagerness for this experience.

I'm going to bring some "things" that we'll spread all over to enrich the experience: creamy whipped cream, sticky honey, sweet-smelling chocolate syrup, flavorful maraschino cherries. I'll lick everything clean with my tongue using long, driving, hard strokes. I'll suck till I get nauseous. You'll have had so much that you won't know whether you're coming or going.

We shall indulge to our hearts' content. After we're done, we'll rest for a while and then go back to it. I'll try to please you any way I can. I haven't had much myself lately, so I think there'll be no stopping me.

Oh, my love. I can't wait. I get excited just writing about it. _____ night, let's do it. Let's go off our diets.
                    DAY

Let's Mate on Our Date

Dear _____,

    Let's mate
    On our date
    There's no debate
    It's our fate
    I anticipate
    It'll be great
    So why wait?
    Don't hesitate
    Eliminate
    Your heart of slate
    Open your gate
    I'll investigate
    You'll reciprocate
    I'll penetrate
    You'll appreciate
    I'll fascinate
    You'll celebrate
    So let's mate
    On our date
    Participate
    If you want to rate!

The Die-Hard's Love Letter

Dear _____,

    For you, my little cupid, my love has no bounds, and no boundaries can contain my love. You are my drug, and I am your addict. Life without you would be incomplete, and I am incomplete without your life.

    There is nothing in the world I wouldn't do for you, and I want you to always remember that. Why, I would gladly give my life to protect you from so much as a scrape on your knee, a windburn on your face, dirt under your toenail. There are so many ways in which I would be only too happy to prove my love for you.

    I love you so much, I could spend the rest of my life with you . . . even if:

- You have a habit of drinking milk and then letting it run out of your nose.
- You undergo a hormonal change which suddenly causes you to give off a nauseating stench.
- You suck . . . peach pits, that is, with your mouth open, when people talk to you.
- You decide you wanna become the other sex.
- You drool in your sleep and dribble when you kiss.
- You begin eating like a pig and become obese.
- You have a lobotomy.

Letter to Give to Your Mate on Your Wedding Day

Dear _____,

Today we march to the gallows! Be brave, poor soul. Crueler fates has history bestowed upon men and women. Allow me a final reflection. I've seen enough late-night TV movies to know that I'm entitled to a few last words.

I didn't know it would end this way, I really didn't. It began innocently enough, but "like" changed to love and love gave way to commitment.

It is true that I am guilty of loving you and pledging to spend the rest of my life with you. But I ask, does such action merit capital punishment? Do these deeds warrant such suffering? Have I committed such a terrible offense? Spare me, Lord! Surely there are people guilty of more heinous crimes who get off much easier.

I suppose I shouldn't feel sorry for myself though. I deserve the fate that awaits me. Many other people have gone to the gallows and were brave about it.

Can you imagine? There will be people present today celebrating our execution. You'd think it was some kind of festival with the music and all. Do you think they'll play "Another One Bites the Dust," or "The Party's Over," or "Gone With the Wind"? Last rites will be delivered by _____.

                                                 NAME OF CLERGYMAN

Well, all I can say is, I hope there's life after death!

Of course, you realize I'm only kidding. This letter is to say that I look forward to a lifetime of happiness with you and wish good health and fortune for us and our family.

Now get ready. The gallows awaits us!

The Gay Love Letter

Dear _____,

Thith ith a tough world for people like uth. But you thure make traveling down life'th old dirt road a real pleathure. I hope I've been thomewhat of a thtimuluth for you too. I feel on top of my world and I want to feel up yourth.

You're very underthanding and I love you for that. You're my biggetht thupporter. At timeth I have a very thriveled opinion of mythelf tho I apprethiate your backing.

Only pleath don't become too pothethive. I love people and have a deep need for lotth of friendth. Tho don't ever athk me to move away with you. I can't leave my buddieth behind.

The "Say 'I Love You'" Love Letter

Dear _____,

This is not a complaint, but you don't say "I love you" often enough to me. It's something I love to hear, because when you say it, I feel good and also reassured. Say I'm insecure, say I'm overromantic, but say it!

I don't think love is anything that should be taken for granted. What's wrong with two people who love each other constantly repeating these 3 little words to their partner? After loving somebody for a long time, people often tend to take their relationship for granted and become taciturn. But the everyday humdrum of a relationship can be avoided if two people really want. Intimate verbal communication is the key. Lovers should always act like two teenagers in the beginning of their first romance.

Just get this giddy beam in your eyes, smile, and then say "I love you." You can practice being "cute" about it in front of the mirror. I'll do the same and together we can be a loving couple. Saying "I love you" is something that should not be saved for special occasions. Life is too short to let something so meaningful be said so scarcely.

You can say it whenever you want (and I hope it will be often), but if you love me, you must agree to this: whenever I tap your lips with my index finger, you shall get a giddy beam in your eyes, smile, and say "I love you!"

Lover's Ticket

```
┌─────────────────────────┐  Ticket No.:_____
│  _____  │
│  NAME                   │  Date of Offense:_____
│  _____  │
│                         │  Place of Offense:_____
│  _____  │
│  ADDRESS                │  Arresting Officer:_____
│  _____  │                  YOUR NAME
│  CITY, STATE, ZIP CODE  │
└─────────────────────────┘
```

_____

Violation (describe in detail):

_____

NOTICE: You are hereby summoned to appear at _____, _____, PLACE   ADDRESS
_____, at _____o'clock on
    TOWN OR CITY   TIME
_____. You will be tried in reference to the
     DATE
above violation. You may plead your case with the assistance of photographs and sketches. Your case will be reviewed by "The Judge" with appropriate action to be taken if proven guilty and a celebration if shown not guilty (you win either way!).

_____
       JUDGE
(Sign your name)

77

The Fairy Tale Love Letter

Dear _____,

Our love is so strong, it's like a storybook romance. As a matter of fact, it reminds me of a fairy tale I once read as a child. It went something like this:

Once upon a time, there was a beautiful young princess named _____ella.
_{FEMALE'S NAME (IF IT ENDS IN A VOWEL, DROP LAST LETTER)}
She was a "closet" princess; for while this title was not official, she possessed all the qualities and goodness of royalty. In reality, she had little money and thus had limited exposure. But all the young men in the land, if given the opportunity to meet her, would undoubtedly fall in love with the divine young belle.

One night, by a stroke of chance, she decided to go to a local "hotspot" called _____. It was
_{CLUB, DISCO OR BAR}
dark and there were many people there. Fate was kind that night, the _____ day of _____,
_{NUMBER}   _{MONTH}
_____, for it brought her together with a "closet"
_{YEAR}
prince. She met a handsome young man named _____. He was a _____
_{NAME}   _{JOB}
by profession and was as charming and romantic as any real prince who ever lived.

Together, they went out to many places: _____, _____,
_{PLACE}   _{PLACE}
_____, and _____ to name
_{PLACE}   _{PLACE}

just a few. They enjoyed each other's company immensely and were very attracted to one another. They soon fell in love, and Prince _____

NAME
asked Princess _____ella to marry him.

NAME
She enthusiastically consented and the wedding date was set for _____. They shortly afterwards be-

DATE
came king and queen in their palace at _____ and were parents of _____

ADDRESS   NUMBER
little princes and princesses. Everybody in the _____ household is now living happily

LAST NAME
ever after.

80

Love Letter to a Celebrity

Dear _____,

You have always been my favorite _____. I remember years ago staying up late at night to _____ your _____. I was so turned on by your _____ that I would have trouble falling asleep because you were still _____ing in my mind.

Your dreamy _____ is enough to make any _____ go off the deep end. How _____ you are! You must have such an exciting life with all the _____ing you do.

If we could only _____, my dreams would come true. I know that I would be different than all those other _____ that write to you. I want to get to know you not for your fame or fortune, but for your _____ and your _____. I'm just sure we would _____ together so well.

I hope that you just don't pass this off as another letter from a _____. I truly want to _____ you. Please write to me. I'll be thinking of you tonight again when I am _____ing.

The Marriage Proposal Love Letter

Dear _____,

 I'ma gonna make ya an offer ya can't a refusa. I a wanta make ya a permanent a part of my a life. I ain't a no good in a writing letters, but I a never proposed to a no girl before and I a don't a get on a my knees for a nobody.

 We been a going togedda now for _____ (NUMBER) _____ (MONTHS/YEARS) and I a know you ain't a ever goin' to a leave me because you a knowa too mucha, so I figured we a might asa well a get hitched. Let me a put it dis way: if you a don't a marry me, I'm a gonna give ya a pair of cement galoshes.

 Now don't go gettin' any ideas—nuttin' will change except you're gonna gimme 3 sons and you'll live comftably for da rest of your natral life, whaddever dat is.

 I a don't a need a no answer from a you. I'm a going to set da date for a _____ (MONTH) _____ (DAY), _____ (YEAR). If you a know a what's good for you, you'll be der. By da way, my a friend, da mayor, is gonna marry us.

Woman's Response to a Marriage Proposal

Dear _____,

This is in reference to your proposition for me to become your wife. A decision has been made. Before I tell you what it is, however, first you should know something about the determination.

The competition was tough. There were 4 candidates who campaigned for this. Selection of the "winner" was based on the judging of various factors as excellent, good, average or poor, as appears below. To protect the names of the innocent, I have designated the other candidates' names with the letters X, Y and Z.

Candidate	Face	Body	Personality	Brains	Kindness	Sexiness
X	Excellent	Average	Average	Excellent	Good	Excellent
Y	Good	Excellent	Excellent	Good	Excellent	Excellent
Z	Average	Average	Good	Average	Good	Average
_____	FILL IN	FILL IN	FILL IN	FILL IN	FILL IN	FILL IN
LOVER'S LAST NAME						

Now you see how you compare to the competition. Based on my opinion, I have to overwhelmingly say that my answer to your question of whether I'll marry you or not is _____.
 YES/NO

85

The Questionnaire Love Letter

Dear _____,

For the period that we've known each other, our communication has been essentially oral. I think there's always more to learn about a person, and one way to get better insight into a person is by having him or her respond on paper to written questions. (One might answer the same question differently in writing than orally.) Thus, I have prepared the following questionnaire which I would appreciate your completing. This will give me more insight into your interests as well as what you don't like, enabling me to plan and act accordingly. Please return this to me after you answer the questions. Thank you.

1. Check off which of the following activities you like to do or places you like to go on dates:

    ____ passion pit (movies)
    ____ horseback riding
    ✓ swimming pool
    ✓ beach
    ____ miniature golf
    ✓ theater (shows)
    ____ parks
    ✓ parking
    ✓ parties
    ____ bowling
    ✓ restaurant
    ✓ pizza parlor
    ✓ ice cream parlor
    ____ wine & cheese restaurant
    ____ discos
    ____ bars
    ____ airports
    ____ rollerskating
    ____ ice skating
    ____ paddleball
    ____ tennis
    ____ checkers
    ____ chess
    ✓ making-out
    ____ other (name them)

87

2. Which of the following do you prefer when having a sexual experience?
   1) tying up your partner
   2) using mayonnaise
   3) using peanut butter and jelly
   4) lying dead and pretending it's necrophilia

3. In 25 words or less, tell why you are so wonderful.

4. If we were married, would you permit your best-looking friend to share an apartment with us if he/she asked? Why or why not?

5. What cartoon character do you most relate to and why?

6. Describe the personality of your ideal man/woman.

7. How do you like a man/woman to dress?

8. Describe your feelings toward sex.

9. If you were marooned on a desert island and could have three things, what would you choose?

10. If you were on a first date with someone and the car you were riding in broke down in an isolated area in the middle of the night, what would you do?

11. Write the word that first comes to your mind after reading each word below:

love_____ horny_____
fun_____ embarrassing_____
baby_____ backseat_____
goofy_____ marriage_____
sex_____ _____ _____
stud_____ elephant balls_____
                            YOUR NAME

12. Circle the adjectives below that you believe most aptly describe you:

warm	prudish	sensitive
snobbish	reserved	intelligent
down-to-earth	emotional	ugly
friendly	compassionate	average-looking
vulnerable	shy	cute
classy	outgoing	beautiful
indifferent	money-hungry	a perfect "10"

13. In one sentence write what you would want to hear most from a man/woman you liked.

14. What are your vices? (Be explicit)

15. Which is your fantasy?

whips and chains_____   a tropical island_____
ménage à trois_____   your mother or father_____
Raquel Welch/Paul   other_____
  Newman_____

16. How would you like to spend your next birthday?

89

17. What gift would you like to give someone you love?
    _____

    What gift would you like to receive from someone you love?_____

18. Describe your "first time."

19. What would you like to be remembered for?

20. What movie star or politician would you most like to spend an evening with? Why?

21. If you were a musical instrument, what would you be? Why?

22. Tell me a secret.

The Nighttime Love Letter

Dear _____,

A person may have difficulty falling asleep if he or she has an overactive _____. Let me ease your
<u>NOUN</u>
_____ tensions with my special advice that
<u>ADJECTIVE</u>
will quickly and efficiently put you into a(n) _____ state.
<u>ADJECTIVE</u>

_____'s Rx for Sleeping:
<u>YOUR NAME</u>

1. Eat a(n) _____ at bedtime. The nutrients from this
   <u>NOUN</u>
   particular food will facilitate a somnolent state. But be sure to avoid _____ and _____ as these
   <u>PLURAL NOUN</u>   <u>PLURAL NOUN</u>
   can be difficult to digest.

2. _____ for one hour before bedtime. This will
   <u>VERB</u>
   help take your mind off those problems that always seem to pop up when you get into bed.

3. Wear a(n) _____. Comfort is the key to fall-
   <u>CLOTHING ARTICLE</u>
   ing asleep. Any tight fits will cause blood to rush to your head and make you _____.
   <u>ADJECTIVE</u>

4. Breathe heavily. Think of _____.
   <u>PERSON'S FAVORITE MOVIE STAR</u>

5. Turn out all lights and close curtains. There should be no interference from the outside world.

6. Think about how _____ you are. Repeat this
   <u>ADJECTIVE</u>
   thought over and over in your mind until you can't take it any more. Then proceed to point #7.

7. Attack me. I'll put you out.

The Romantic Love Letter

Dear _____,

    There's nothing more I'd rather do than sit under the stars with you on some tropical island, sipping _____ and holding your hand as an ocean
_{BEVERAGE}
breeze gently cools us off.

    The scenario would be very romantic: we would have a cozy little table on the beach with _____ on
_{PLURAL NOUN}
it. Around us would be white sand and green palm trees. You'd be wearing your evening _____ and
_{CLOTHING ARTICLE}
I'd have on my _____. In the background a
_{CLOTHING ARTICLE}
little band would softly be playing "_____."
_{NAME OF SONG}

    All your problems would go away, and the only thing on your mind would be _____. We would
_{NOUN}
watch the starlit ocean and see the waves come roaring into shore. The world would seem to exist only for the two of us, and it would be the most exalted evening of your life. It would be a dream come true that you would never want to end. Tingles of joy and chills of ecstasy would travel up and down your spine. You'd be gazing dreamily into my eyes and, in the most passionate of moments, lean over and whisper into my ear "_____!"
_{STATEMENT}

Love Letter to a Guy Who Becomes Cheap

Dear _____,

I've noticed lately a serious cut in your offense budget. We've been eating at diners instead of restaurants, going to the movies instead of the theater, taking buses instead of driving or taking cabs. Such policy is of serious concern to my national welfare.

In this day and age, one must appropriate a sufficient budget for maneuvering. How can he expect to cultivate healthy relations with another nation without expending the right amount of aid? When aid is cut off, the party which has been spoiled can easily become apathetic or even belligerent.

I realize the cost of services and supplies has increased, but everyone is susceptible to such increases. And I observe, with much envy, that my neighboring comrades haven't suffered any due to inflation.

So heed this bulletin, my friend. Reinstate your old strategy. Make peace, not war. Keep the natives happy, and they'll make you happy too.

A Single Person's Love Letter to a Non-Expressive Partner

Dear _____,

We've been going together for _____ now.
_{LENGTH OF TIME}
During this time, we have shared many details about our lives. But neither of us has been very emotional or expressed our intimate feelings to the other.

I've been waiting for you to tell me something, anything, but you haven't said a word yet. Sometimes I think you're about to because I can see it in your eyes. But now my emotions are too intense, my passions are boiling at too high a flame to hold back from saying what I feel. So what if you haven't said anything to me? I'm not exactly sure how you feel, but I know how I do. Why should I not express myself because you haven't said anything yet? Why should I let silly pride get in the way? I must tell you, now, how I feel. I can't hold back any longer: I'm madly in . . . *like* . . . with you!

The "Fruity" Person's Love Letter After the First Sexual Experience

Dear _____Sharon_____,

Well, squeeze my lemons! We finally made it; you ate the forbidden fruit. I hope it was sweet enough for you. It had a long enough time to ripen.

I want you to know that my mangos are always in season. You'll see that they're plump and juicy all year round. Whenever you want a delightful refreshment, take a bite and swallow. Ahhhhhh . . . delicious.

I'd like to plant my banana tree in your garden. If you tell me you can't because of a periodic flood then I'll feel very melon-choly because I'll think you're full of prunes. That's the best time to fertilize a garden.

P.S. Kiss my cantaloupes!

Letter to Your Secret Lover

Dear _____,

    I have enjoyed our game of love but am tired of playing second-string quarterback. When you first told me you already had a starter, I thought, okay, maybe you would eventually change the lineup. Just wait till you saw my talents!

    I quickly found out you were as much a sports fanatic as I was. Together, we have made a great team, playing every position on offense and defense. We have scored so many touchdowns that I've lost track. We've played night games, morning games, afternoon games—anytime or anywhere you've wanted. You seem pleased but always take me out to return to your original lineup. How do you think that makes me feel? I'm sitting on the bench while you're out there playing on the field.

    I was foolish to be taken in by your insincere flattery, telling me how great a player I am. I love the attention and praise you shower upon me, but I will not be blinded by your passes.

    I think you've used me. You really don't want me. I'm just a plaything for you. Well, I've come to my senses now and am not going to stand for this anymore. Put me in the starting lineup or the ball game's over!

Love Letter to Use After an Argument

Dear _____,

 As chief military advisor of _____ (YOUR ADDRESS), it is my duty to look into the _____-_____ (RECIPIENT'S FIRST NAME) (YOUR FIRST NAME) crisis and negotiate a peaceful settlement. These two nations have traditionally enjoyed happy and peaceful relations, and it is my sincere hope that they will continue to do so.

 It is easy in today's world for two countries to blow up at each other or in severe cases to declare war. While ideally nations coexist, simultaneously receiving and giving aid to each other, the pressures and tensions of the outside world sometimes become overbearing and contribute to the outbreak of war with the slightest disagreement between two countries.

 Think of the squabble. Is it anything two developed, mature and intelligent nations can't solve? Is it that important in the overall scheme of things that it should separate the two of you and keep you from enjoying harmonious relations? Is it worth all the happiness you've built and time and understanding you two have put into one another?

Let's sit down and talk this thing over. I'm sure we can come to a satisfactory agreement. A successful negotiation will be celebrated at your favorite restaurant with a special fireworks display put on later in the evening in your honor.

_____
SECRETARY OF LOVE

The Lusty Guy's Love Letter

Dear _____,

You say that when it comes to sex, I am an animal. That I treat you like a piece of dirt and really don't give a hopping shit about you—that just as long as I have a hole, any hole, to get my rocks off, I'd be satisfied. And that you're disgusted by my vile and putrid language, telling me I'm as low a life as lowlives can be. On top of all this, you even call me a "phony," a Doctor Jekyll and Mr. Hyde who is real nice in front of other people but a vermin with you alone.

With this in mind, my angel, my sweet little cherub, my delicate femme, I want you to read this letter which has been inspired by the passions of my heart. My dear, I apologize for the crude behavior I have exhibited, for deep down I am a gentle and compassionate soul. I, too, concur that the union of two people is a sacred thing of life which should be approached with love and respect. A man should treat a woman with tenderness, for that is the essence of her nature, and she will willingly reciprocate. A relationship is best served when this is the thread that bonds the two together. Be a kind and understanding human being and realize that I am only a victim of the condition called "man" and that my good senses are overwhelmed by the physical beauty which you are.

Now, I hope you've had enough of this pork poetry, you bitch, because I'm as horny as a motherfucker and want to stick my meat into your oven!

The Ego-Booster Love Letter

Dear _____,

    Mere words cannot express the joy and happiness I get from you. To know the real _____ is to experience one of life's greatest joys.

NAME

    You posess so many wonderful qualities that it's hard to believe that such a person really exists. You are, in the truest sense of these words: compassionate, kind, considerate, caring, sensitive, understanding, affectionate, romantic, elegant, devoted, and precious. Sometimes I think you must be part of a dream I'm having because you're too good to be true.

    I mean all this with all my heart. You know I love you deeply and would do anything in the world for you. But I love you the way I do for the reasons I've written. So remember, I'll always be there for you if you need me.

    I hope this letter has lifted your spirits. If you ever need anything else boosted, just let me know. I'll be happy—or should I say excited—to do it!

The Suggestive Love Letter

Dear _____,

   I think it's healthy for lovers to have fantasies. Making love is wonderful, but no matter how much two people love each other, lovemaking usually does become routine after a while. Concocting zany and wild fantasies is fun and beneficial and below appear some of mine. I'd like to know some of yours.

1. I'd like to be your dessert smorgasbord. You would put whipped cream on my legs, chocolate mousse on my arms, tapioca pudding on my chest, Jell-O on my stomach, and peanut butter on my crotch (peanut butter because it takes longer to munch).
2. I'd like to be locked with you in a freezer and be kept warm by your using electrically heated gloves.
3. I would like to sleep on a mattress with a big hole in it around the buttocks region. You would be lying face up underneath it and me face down on top.
4. You would shrink yourself to about two inches in height and then go mountain climbing on my unclothed body. (Feel free to camp out in my dark forest region.)
5. I would like to go sit-down surfing with you as my hard and stiff surfboard.

The Smitten Person's Letter

Dear _____,

    I'm sure you're aware that everything's got to come to an end sometime. Nothing is forever.

    Thus, I am suggesting that you end it all now. Sure it's been fun, but why live under the anxiety that one day your number's going to be up anyway? Who needs that pressure?

    You're young, but you've lived a full life. You're healthy, but sooner or later, it hits us. There's no dodging it. Some people will miss you, but you can't expect that to be a deterrent. Think of it not as the end of the world, only the end of life, as you know it. Get it over with. Don't prolong the agony.

    Let me help you end it. There are many ways to go. Some hopeless victims have been known to jump out of an airplane, others have been pushed down the plank. I'll leave the choice up to you.

    Please, I beg you. Do it! Do it now. You won't regret it.

    Marry me!

Love Letter to Give to Someone on the Street Whom You Are Attracted To

Hi there!

Please forgive my forwardness in presenting this letter to you and take a few minutes to read it. It will mean a great deal to me.

This might sound crazy, but when I saw you just now I couldn't believe my eyes. You are the most _____ person I ever saw. I'm sure that
_{GORGEOUS/HANDSOME}
your intelligence, sensitivity, and charm complement your ethereal beauty. You must be a very special person.

No, I am not a crackpot or anything of the sort. Just a real romantic _____. My friends think I'm kind and
_{GUY/GAL}
gentle. I'm a(n) _____.
_{JOB OR PROFESSION}

By the way, my name is _____.
_{NAME}

The fact that I had this letter does not mean that I carry letters like this around all the time and hand them out whenever I see attractive _____. This is my
_{WOMEN/MEN}
one and only letter. I've always thought that one day I'd see the _____ of my dreams walking on the street, as
_{GIRL/GUY}
I have when I saw you, and I wanted to be prepared. I am too shy to start a conversation with a stranger, and you never meet the "right" people in singles' bars, so I didn't want to take any chance in letting you walk out of my life.

I'd really like to meet you. I know it's crazy, but why don't you give it a chance? No one will believe this, and one day we might even laugh about it.

If you are interested in giving "us" a try, call me at _____ (TELEPHONE NUMBER) or drop me a line at _____ (ADDRESS). If you are married or otherwise involved, please pass this on to your best-looking available friend.

The Mae West Love Letter

Hi there, Big _____,
_{NAME (FIRST SYLLABLE ONLY)}

Congratulations! Your recent performance entitles you to play the big part in my life story. The competition was tough, but you certainly tried the hardest.

Since we'll be rehearsing together frequently in the coming weeks, I thought we ought to get to know each other better. I have the script, and believe me, there's a lot for you to go over. I require my leading men to give command performances each time. Don't worry about over-rehearsing. Too much of a good thing is wonderful.

I'd like you to acquaint yourself with the enclosed script. Then when you come here to meat (sic) me and rehearse, we can improvise. Use your imagination and think up some devilish ideas. Between two evils, I always pick the one I never tried before. If you're fresh, be careful. I generally avoid temptation until I see it.

If you perform in our rehearsals as well as you did in the tryouts, then I'll be your biggest booster. Don't worry about me. When I'm good, I'm very good, but when I'm bad, I'm better. You may have heard about all the men in my life. Just remember, it's the life in my men that counts!

As far as acting is concerned, take this bit of advice: It isn't what you do but how you do it. It isn't what you feel but how you feel it. Just do what you feel and feel what you do and look good when you do it and feel it!

Why don't you come up
and see me sometime,

Letter to a Jewish Mother

Dear Mom,

I have something very heavy to say to you that I thought would be best expressed in a letter, especially since I never seem to be able to get *my* point across to you when speaking, anyway. I'm afraid you're not going to like what I have to say, so you better sit down.

I'm moving out of home, Ma. I think it's about time. I'm _____ years old and all my friends have their
_{NUMBER}

own apartments. Some are even married and have families, like you and Dad!

Don't try to talk me out of it this time. My mind is made up! But don't worry. I can take care of myself out of your home. As a matter of fact, I feel so guilty about moving out that I've made up a list of promises to keep so you won't worry about me so much.

I promise:
1. to have everyone take off their shoes before entering my home;
2. to cover all my new furniture and not let anyone sit on it;
3. not to eat *traif* out;
4. to always ride in cars with the doors locked;
5. to open the door to men's (women's) rooms by

having only my pinky come in contact with the door handle so I won't get my hand dirty;
6. to put toilet paper on all public toilets before going;
7. not to develop any more *mishagoses*;
8. not to schlep around anything heavy;
9. not to date shikses (shaigetzes);
10. never to reveal your real age;
11. to wait at least three hours after eating meat to have ice cream, milk, or any other dairy product;
12. to place a mezuzah at the entrance to every door in my home and kiss it each time I enter;
13. to buy only large cars so if I have an accident I can't get hurt too badly;
14. to clean my house at every possible moment of my spare time and hire a maid to come in at least once a week;
15. to uphold the myth, when I get married, that Jewish men (women) make the best husbands (wives);
16. to make my children feel guilty for any illogical behavior (I can use some of your lines: "Your dinner's getting cold. Come in right away." "You're killing me!");
17. to teach my children, when they're ready to get married, that there's no one good enough for them around;
18. to continue your rent support.

        Goodbye till next Friday night's Shabbas dinner and don't worry about me,

The Stop-Playing-Games Love Letter

Dear _____,

    You love to play games so much that I've got one for you. It's called "Simon Says." You've played it before, but now it counts for real. Here goes:

Simon says plan ahead—don't make last-minute plans.
Simon says keep your word when you promise something.
Simon says stop lying to me.
Simon says express your true emotional feelings about me.
Simon says don't make excuses for things you'd really like to do with me.
Simon says be loving.
Simon says he's got a game for you.
Simon says extend your arms out.
Simon says put your arms around me.
Simon says hold me tight.
Simon says kiss me.
Simon says get ready.
Simon says here goes . . .
Simon says stop playing games!

Getting Your Lover to Change

Dear _____,

During the period of our relationship, we have grown to care about each other in a very special way. While we have made certain pledges to one another, we still lack a total commitment, and I know you're out there "doing it." I urge you to give this up immediately.

This could not only be unhealthy for, but fatal to, our relationship. It pains me greatly to know you would want to sneak behind my back to do it. Feeling about you the way I do, I couldn't bring myself to do it. I'd rather sit here dreaming about you.

If we're going to make it (and I certainly hope we do), you're going to have to get your act together. Stop now before it's too late. Smoking can be dangerous to your health!

P.S. It makes kissing you less enjoyable also, as it leaves your breath smelling stinky!

The Real Man's Letter

Dear _____,

    I'm what they call a Real Man. They're tough, potent, rugged. There's some things you should know about Real Men:

Real Men don't wear bikini underwear. They wear white Jockey shorts.
Real Men don't like women who "submit" too readily. Half the fun is in the chase.
Real Men don't rush sex. They keep their women in suspense.
Real Men can hold back from "coming" for at least four hours.
Real Men don't fantasize.
Real Men enjoy oral sex.
A Real Man *always* brings a woman to orgasm.
Real Men don't make sounds or scratch backs.
Real Men keep on going after orgasm.
Real Men don't use lubricants, vibrators, or artificial devices.
Real Men don't screw women "on the rag."
Real Men don't get herpes or VD. They don't sleep with sluts.
This is not a love letter.
Real Men don't write love letters.

The "Love at First Sight" Letter

Dear _____,

When we first met, it was "love at first sight" for me. How did I know this? Well, I've composed this little poem that will tell you:

My heart went boom
And my eyes went zoom
And I didn't know if it
   was day or night
I was dazzled by your smile
And beguiled by your style
Oh me! I thought, this could
   only be love at first sight

You were everything I wanted
What for years I had hunted
But could never find any place
   at all
I searched every nook and cranny
And I even asked my granny
If the order I had wanted was
   too tall

She said, "No, child, don't worry
And don't be in a hurry
True love is just a real hard
   thing to find
When you'll see your love, you'll
   know
Cause your heart will be aglow
And that will put you in a wild
   state of mind"

When I met you I went crazy
And everything was hazy
I was blinded by the shining
   light of love
I thought I was in heaven
Yet I felt like I was seven
Ah, you must have been a gift
   from up above

When I first saw your face
I said I must now reach
   first base
And kiss your nose and neck
   and cheeks and forehead too
The rest would come sometime
There was no need to rush
   the time
For this was only going to be
   our debut

You were the essence of
   perfection
I found out upon inspection
In the first five seconds of
   the time I looked
I knew you'd want some time
If I asked you to be mine
But I knew that I was already
   hooked!

I submerged my defenses
I guess I lost my senses
I felt like a stick of dynamite
I was a different person—uh oh!
So I guess that's how I just
   know
That I fell in love with you
   at first sight!

Woman's Letter to a Lecher

Dear _____,

Our sexual activity is leaving me exhausted and sore. Every night, bang, bang, bang; all you want is sex, sex, and more sex. The only thing you seem to have on your mind is ravishing, and nothing can satisfy your physical appetite. I can't take it any longer.

Some nights you "go easy" on me and assume the standard position. But other times you want me to fulfill all your fantasies: "doggie" style, standing up, on my side, from the rear, bending over, on the kitchen table.

Well . . . here's something new I'd like you to try: Sit on it!